Full Throttle

Bugatti

Tracy Nelson Maurer

Rourke
Publishing LLC
Vero Beach, Florida 32964

www.rourkepublishing.com

PHOTO CREDITS: Page 27: © Associated Press, Tammie Arroyo; All other images courtesy Bugatti Motors. www.bugatti.com

Project Assistance: Richard Day, Curator, The Bugatti Trust.

Also, the author extends appreciation to Julie Lundgren, Mike Maurer, Lois M. Nelson, and the team at Rourke Publishing.

Editor: Robert Stengard-Olliges
Page Design: Tara Raymo

Notice: The publisher recognizes that some words, model names, and designations mentioned herein are the property of the trademark holder. They are used for identification purposes only. This is not an official publication.

Library of Congress Cataloging-in-Publication Data

Maurer, Tracy, 1965-
  Bugatti / Tracy Nelson Maurer.
     p. cm. -- (Full throttle 2)
  Includes bibliographical references and index.
  ISBN 978-1-60044-570-5
  1. Bugatti automobile--Juvenile literature. I. Title.
  TL215.B82M38 2008
  629.222--dc22
                               2007014441

Printed in the USA

IG/IG

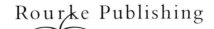

www.rourkepublishing.com – rourke@rourkepublishing.com
Post Office Box 3328, Vero Beach, FL 32964

Table of Contents

The Legend of La Marque

The Bugatti 16.4 Veyron blew away the top speeds for **production cars** when it cruised past 250 miles per hour (400 kilometers per hour).

It blew away acceleration records when it hit 0 to 60 mph (100 km/h) in only 2.5 seconds.

It blew away the know-it-alls who said a street-legal car could not hit 1000 horsepower when the 16-cylinder motor roared over their mark.

But perhaps the Veyron's best performance yet was when it blew the dust off a legendary **marque** in automobile history.

Ettore Bugatti was born in Italy in 1881. He showed early promise as an artist like his father, Carlo. Ettore's design talents later blended with his stronger mechanical abilities to create masterpieces in automobile styling and engineering.

Ettore Bugatti built his first racecar at age 18.

marque
> the logo or brand for an automobile manufacturer or its models

production car
> a car built for sale to the public

Fäst Fäct

Ettore called his Type 10 *Pur Sang*, meaning "thoroughbred."

From 1899 to 1909, Ettore designed cars for other manufacturers, including the Bugatti Types 1 to 9. He also worked on personal projects, such as his Types 2 and 8. By 1910, Ettore opened his own factory at Molsheim, Germany.

Le Patron Rules

In 1914, World War I forced Ettore and his young family to flee to France. The French-speaking Bugattis lived well there. Ettore continued to design new motors, such as a powerful 16-cylinder airplane engine.

Many nations' boundaries changed after the war ended in 1918. The Bugatti factory was now part of France instead of Germany. Ettore gladly returned. He reigned over his company like a fatherly, but picky king. The French called him "Le Patron," meaning "The Boss."

Some Bugatti Racing Innovations

- **1922** Cigar body shape on the Type 29/30
- **1923** Ground-hugging covered wheels and curved body on the Type 32 "Tank"
- **1924** Lightweight aluminum alloy wheels with eight spokes on the Type 35

"La Marque"—as the French called the car company—became the pride of France, even if Bugatti was an Italian.

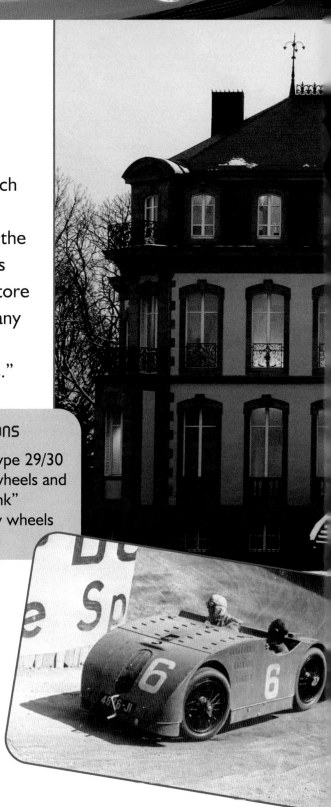

grand prix
French words meaning "big prize"; the fastest racing series, like the modern Formula One

restoration
returning something to its former condition

The historic Chateau St. Jean was where Ettore Bugatti once met with his elite customers and rode horses. The preserved stable buildings now house reception and meeting areas, a library, and a **restoration** workshop.

In the years between the World Wars, Bugatti racecars swept the checkered flag thousands of times! They mostly entered the European **grand prix** races. From 1925 to 1929, Bugattis won the rugged Targa Florio road race five straight times. This unpaved route snaked through the mountains of Italy for more than 67 tricky miles (108 km).

7

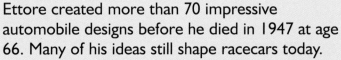

The Clever Competitor

How did Bugattis claim thousands of victories? Ettore's early concern for **aerodynamic** and lightweight designs made his cars fast. He was also a clever competitor. Back then, manufacturers sponsored factory teams. Bugatti changed the racing world forever by selling Type 35s built to racing **specifications** to private drivers. These early privateers entered their cars in countless grand prix races and made Bugatti famous around the world.

Ettore created more than 70 impressive automobile designs before he died in 1947 at age 66. Many of his ideas still shape racecars today.

For safety, early drivers and their mechanics wore leather gloves, soft leather helmets, and goggles. No seat belts. No roll bars. Not even windshields. Many drivers died in crashes.

aerodynamic
shaped for air to flow easily over the body at higher speeds

specifications
detailed design instructions or a list of these technical features

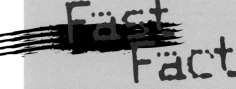

Until 1925, a mechanic rode beside the driver during the race.

History Drives the Future

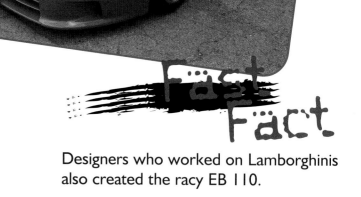

Ettore Bugatti's company built its last car in 1961. Racing fans and car buffs never forgot his winning racecars and fancy touring cars. Several businessmen tried to bring back the Bugatti marque between the 1960s and 1990s. A few **concept cars** and brief production runs, such as the one for the EB 110, kept "Bugattistes" hopeful.

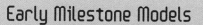

Designers who worked on Lamborghinis also created the racy EB 110.

Early Milestone Models

- **1901** Type 2 became the first winning Bugatti car
- **1921** Type 13 swept the top four places at the Voiturettes Grand Prix in Brescia
- **1924** Type 35 won more races than any other racecar ever
- **1928** Type 41 Royale designed as the most expensive automobile for the times
- **1934** Type 57 proved son Jean's talents; variations won at Le Mans in 1937 and 1939

Type 50

concept car
a vehicle built to try out new looks and techniques

Fast Fact

Just over 100 of the EB 100s rolled out of the factory.

Romano Artioli owned the Bugatti car marque in the early 1990s. He unveiled the EB 110 GT on September 15, 1991 to honor Ettore Bugatti's 110th birthday. The EB 110's 560 hp V-12 engine topped out at about 208 mph (336 km/h). The car was fast, but sales were slow. Bugatti operations closed—again—in 1995.

Revival Milestones

- **1991** EB 110 revived the Bugatti supercar
- **1993** EB 112 sedan concept honored the stylish Type 57 Atlantic
- **1998** EB 118 concept featured a W-18 and recalled the swooped 1931 Type 50
- **1999** EB 218 sedan limousine concept sported a W-18 front engine and dorsal groove
- **1999** Bugatti 18/3 Chiron sports car concept claimed a 555-hp, 18 cylinder engine
- **1999** Bugatti 18/4 Veyron supercar concept unveiled with a W-18 engine
- **2005** Bugatti 16.4 Veyron supercar released as the world's fastest, most expensive, and most powerful production car

The "-est" Car

If the Veyron is now the future of supercars, it's because of its past. The Volkswagen AG (VW) automobile powerhouse bought the Bugatti marque in 1998 and opened Bugatti Automobiles S.A.S. in 2000. The company set a goal to honor Bugatti's history with an "-e-s-t" production car. Coolest. Smartest. Fastest. Quickest. Toughest to achieve, but Ettore Bugatti expected only the best—the ultimate "-est."

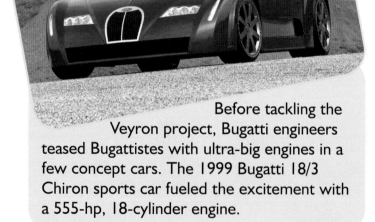

Car buffs called Bugattis "Bugs" long before Americans nicknamed the 1960s Volkswagen Beetles "Bugs."

Pierre Veyron (1903-1970) drove for the Bugatti team that won the 1939 Le Mans 24-hour endurance grand prix race.

Before tackling the Veyron project, Bugatti engineers teased Bugattistes with ultra-big engines in a few concept cars. The 1999 Bugatti 18/3 Chiron sports car fueled the excitement with a 555-hp, 18-cylinder engine.

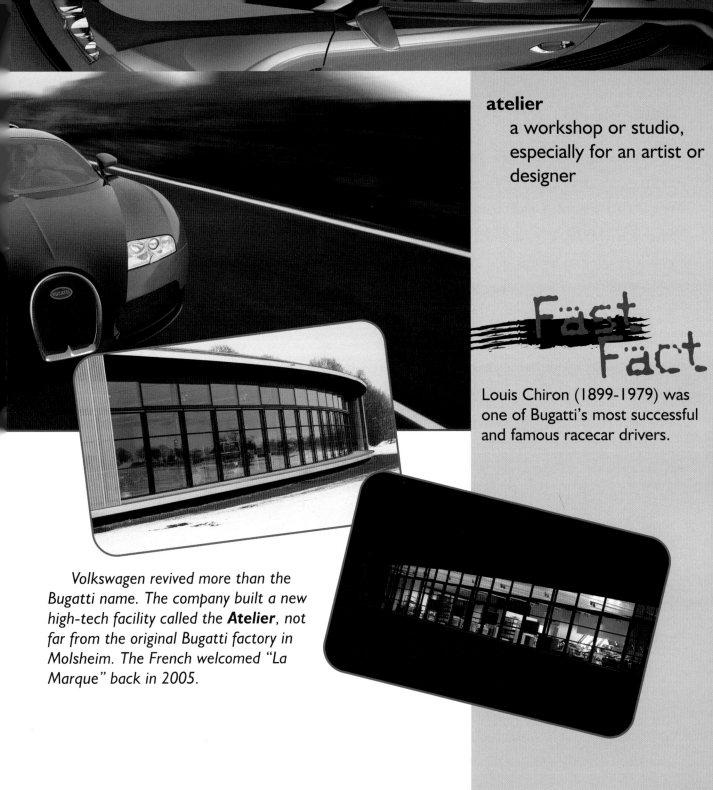

atelier
> a workshop or studio, especially for an artist or designer

Fast Fact

Louis Chiron (1899-1979) was one of Bugatti's most successful and famous racecar drivers.

*Volkswagen revived more than the Bugatti name. The company built a new high-tech facility called the **Atelier**, not far from the original Bugatti factory in Molsheim. The French welcomed "La Marque" back in 2005.*

Told You So

The Bugatti EB 18/4 Veyron concept car with 18 cylinders first took the stage at the Tokyo Motor Show in 1999. Making the dream car a reality took longer than expected. More concept cars and **prototypes** followed. Rumors swirled that the Veyron's huge engine overheated easily and the car didn't handle well at high speeds. In 2003, a prototype Veyron spun out of control at a show. The know-it-alls chirped, "Told you so."

Car experts say that Volkswagen's total project costs divided by the mere 300 Veyrons to be produced put each vehicle's actual cost at about $5 to $6 million.

The biggest challenges?

- Build a 1001 hp engine to fit into a street-legal body
- Cool the powerful engine
- Handle the car at high speeds
- Stop the speedster
- Style the car inside and out to honor Bugatti

prototype
for carmakers, the first working model of a design

Money wasn't a challenge. The Veyron's price tag is about $1.4 million, the world's most expensive production car so far. Bugatti has held the record before. The deluxe Type 41 Royale limousine sold for about $30,000 in 1928 (about $337,300 in today's dollars). A collector sold his Royale in 1987 for nearly $11 million, the highest price ever for an auctioned car.

The Wow of a W-16

True to the Bugatti spirit, the Veyron pushed engine design far ahead of other cars. Volkswagen wanted a 1001 hp motor. Engineers delivered it by merging two V-8s into a very rare W-16. That's W as in Wow! The engineers also put four valves on each cylinder and used four **turbochargers** to stuff more air into the combustion chambers. This helped to double the 8.0-liter engine's output.

The Veyron's engine computer controls the shifting as in a Formula 1 racecar. No clutch. No grinding gears. In just 0.2 seconds, it smoothly shifts gears with only a slight change in the engine purr.

Burning gasoline in the W-16 actually generates about 3000 hp, but about 2000 hp turns into heat. To keep the engine cool, engineers placed it behind the driver without a cover. A huge radiator and nine other parts work to chill the temperatures, too.

Fast Fact

The 8.0-liter Dodge Viper kicks out only about half the horsepower of the 8.0-liter Veyron.

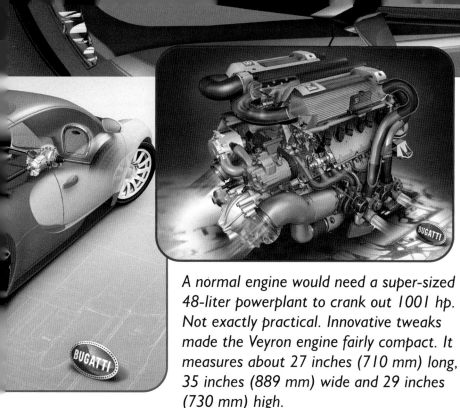

A normal engine would need a super-sized 48-liter powerplant to crank out 1001 hp. Not exactly practical. Innovative tweaks made the Veyron engine fairly compact. It measures about 27 inches (710 mm) long, 35 inches (889 mm) wide and 29 inches (730 mm) high.

turbocharger
a special fan turned by the engine's exhaust gases that works to pump more air into the cylinders and boost power output

Fast Fact

Formula 1 racecars top out around 220 mph (350 km/h)—pokey compared to the Veyron.

The Veyron gets about 19 miles per gallon (8 km/l) on the highway and 4 mpg (1.7 km/l) at top speed. A driver can cruise at the 250-mph (400 km/h) top speed for less than 15 minutes before guzzling all 26.4 gallons (100 liters) in the fuel tank. That's still longer than most roller-coaster rides and soooo much more fun!

Fast Fact

At 1001 hp, the engine burns about 1.33 gallons (5 liters) of gasoline per minute.

17

Smart airflow systems add to Veyron's wow factor. Air cools the engine and feeds the 16 hungry combustion chambers. At top speed, the W-16 gobbles up 45,000 liters of air per minute. Two snorkels at the roofline suck air into the engine. Vents on the rear deck and air scoops along the sides also send air to the engine and rear brakes.

The Veyron's curvy body shape slices through the air. But at over 100 mph (160 km/h), the car can actually lift off the road like an airplane. The Veyron's underbody channels help it stick to the pavement.

Mode	Speed	Clearance	Airflow
Standard	Up to 137 mph (220 km//h)	4.9 inches (12.4 cm)	Underbody channels
Handling	Up to 233 mph (375 km/h)	3.1 inches (7.9 cm) front and 3.7 inches (9.4 cm) rear	Underbody channels + Rear wing
Top Speed (special key required)	Over 234 mph (377 km/h)	2.6 inches (6.6 cm) front and 2.8 inches (7.1 cm) rear	Front diffusers close; Underbody channels + Rear wing

Three driving modes automatically adjust the car's aerodynamics and **suspension** for better handling. When the car hits 137 mph (220 km/h), the rear wing, or spoiler, adds **downforce**. The nose also drops then. Rear diffusers that look like upright gills smooth the underbody airflow for greater control, too.

downforce
  a downward aerodynamic pressure

suspension
  in a vehicle, the system of shock absorbers, springs, and other parts between the wheel and frame that smoothes the ride and increases control

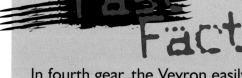

In fourth gear, the Veyron easily passes the liftoff speed for a 747 jet.

The Veyron's lowered suspension isn't new to Bugatti. The Type 57S car that won the 1937 Le Mans had a slinky posture. The "S" stood for "surbaissé," meaning "lowered." Ettore's son Jean designed the car. He later died test-driving it.

19

Achieving the 1001 hp goal meant the engine delivered a whopping 922 lbs.-ft. of torque. A Hummer H1 Alpha tops out at about 520 lbs.-ft. of **torque**. The Veyron needed full-time all-wheel drive to harness all of its power.

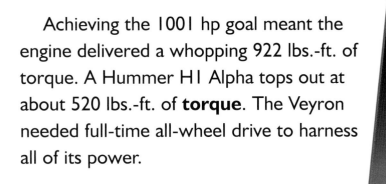

Special carbon-ceramic brakes stop the Veyron from 80 mph (129 km/h) to 0 in just under 200 feet. The system also uses the rear wing like a parachute to help it brake at speeds above 124 mph (200 km/h). The spoiler shifts forward for extra drag.

torque
>   a measure of mechanical strength or turning force

Fast Fact

Racing-style brakes can halt the Veyron from 250 mph (402 km/h) to 0 in about 10 seconds.

Veyron buyers can upgrade to the run-flat PAX system for an additional $43,000. Michelin claims these tires can run flat for about 125 miles (201 km) at 50 mph (80 km/h). The system alerts the driver to loss of tire pressure. The real bonus? No hefty spare tire needed.

The Veyron's $uper Tires:

- Extra-strong
- Heat-resistant
- Road-gripping traction
- Cost about $17,000 for a set

Michelin developed special tires just for the Veyron. The 14.4 inches (365 mm) rear tires ride on 20-inch (508-mm) rims. They're the widest ever produced for a passenger car.

21

Signature Style

The Veyron pays tribute to Bugatti's style with every road-hugging curve. Just two inches narrower than the Hummer H1, the Veyron commands the highway at 79 inches (200 cm) wide and 176 inches (447 cm) long. But it slips under the wind at only 48 inches (122 cm) high. Perfect for handling high speeds.

The horseshoe-shaped grille on the Veyron echoes Ettore Bugatti's design signature. The Veyron also features the hallmark Bugatti two-tone paint style.

monocoque
in vehicles, a body constructed with the frame as a single unit

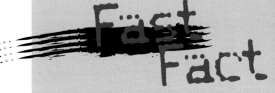

The titanium exhaust ports look cool and stand up to the engine's heat.

The subtle front-to-back center groove on the Veyron recalls the jazzy Type 57 Atlantic's dorsal fin seam.

Ettore Bugatti focused on lightweight designs. He probably would have approved of the Veyron's strong but lightweight parts. A carbon-fiber **monocoque** *structure and aluminum bumpers lighten the load. Still, the car weighs a rather chunky 4,300 pounds (1,950 kg).*

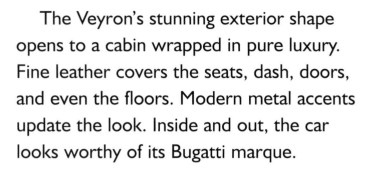

The Veyron's stunning exterior shape opens to a cabin wrapped in pure luxury. Fine leather covers the seats, dash, doors, and even the floors. Modern metal accents update the look. Inside and out, the car looks worthy of its Bugatti marque.

The stereo system rocks! Well insulated to reduce the engine growl and road noise, the cabin is a personal concert hall on wheels.

What's not to like inside the car? It's nearly perfect, but the huge front tires cramp the space inside for passengers' feet.

As expected for a Bugatti, the car's cabin features the latest technical gadgets. Drivers can check each tire's pressure, send data to the Bugatti service team, and plan a trip with the onboard map system.

Nobody accidentally goes over 233 mph (375 km/h) in a Veyron. The driver must use a special key to put the car into Top Speed mode. Then the Veyron adjusts itself for easier handling. The know-it-alls discovered that drivers don't need racing experience to tame this speedster.

Fast Fact

The Veyron is the only car yet with a horsepower dial on its dash that goes up to 1001.

The Supercar of Supercars

Bugatti Automobile SaS planned to build (by hand, of course) about 200 to 350 Veyrons. That's it. More than 100 buyers placed orders even before the cars were ready for production. The Veyron dusted off the Bugatti marque and created new Bugattistes around the world. Many are just now learning about the Bugatti history—and its exciting potential for the future of supercars.

Many Bugatti car clubs have formed worldwide. The Bugatti Owners' Club in England shares the same location as the Bugatti Trust. The Bugatti Trust helps to preserve and share the Bugatti legacy by publishing and collecting books, photographs, and other resources related to the Bugatti marque.

Car collectors appreciate the function and form of Bugatti cars. Experts estimate that only about 700 cars built during Ettore Bugatti's reign still exist today. Although countless car buffs adore the Bugatti marque, a small number worldwide can afford the budget-breaking price tags.

One Bugatti collector is truly qualified to drive his car: Formula 1 champion Michael Schumacher. His Bugatti EB110 could top 200 mph (320 km/h).

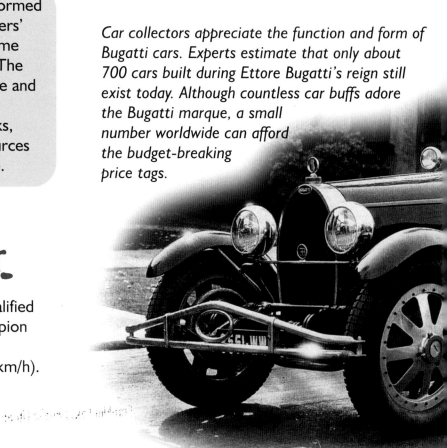

Fashion designer Ralph Lauren collects classic cars. He seems especially fond of Bugattis. More than once, his entries at the elite Pebble Beach **Concours d'Elegance** have won Best of Show.

Concours d'Elegance
an elite show of vintage or classic motor vehicles in original condition

The Bugatti Owners' Club and the Bugatti Trust host events that showcase all models of Bugatti cars.

Who can afford to plunk down over a million dollars to own a Veyron? Business owners, sports stars, car collectors, and movie stars own the primo supercar. Some of the reported new Bugatti owners include:
- Actor Tom Cruise
- Fashion designer Ralph Lauren
- The wife of Volkswagen's former president, Ferdinand Piëch
- Australian soccer player Tim Cahill
- Hip-hop music producer Scott Storch

Ettore Bugatti's legendary work brought beauty to engineering. His designs for automobiles, trains, boats, and airplanes inspired new ways of thinking about high-speed transportation. People still study his ideas today.

The Bugatti Institute of Art, Design and Engineering at England's Coventry University teaches future designers. Computerized equipment and tools allow students to build full-size vehicles in the school's shop. Students are already winning awards for their projects.

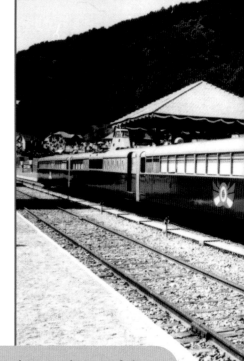

Bugatti designed one of the first high-speed trains. In 1934, the train set a record speed of 122 mph (196 km/h).

Ettore's younger brother Rembrandt became a famous sculptor in Paris in the early 1900s. His 1904 "Standing Playing Elephant" sculpture inspired the solid silver mascot topping the Royale's radiator cap in 1928. Art collectors prize Rembrandt's work just like car collectors treasure Ettore's gems.

Toy companies sell collectible life-like miniatures of the classic Bugatti cars. A "Transformer" toy even morphed into a version of the Veyron.

The Bugatti Circuit in Le Mans, France, honors Ettore Bugatti today. The famous 24 Hours of Le Mans race uses several sections of the track. The Bugatti Circuit is a fitting tribute to the man whose grand prix victories made a lasting "marque" in automobile history.

Glossary

aerodynamic (ahr oh dih NAM ik) – shaped for air to flow easily over the body at higher speeds

atelier (ah TEL yay) – a workshop or studio, especially for an artist or designer

Concours d'Elegance (kohn KUR day lay GAHNS) – an elite show of vintage or classic motor vehicles in original condition

concept car (KAHN sept KAR) – a vehicle built to try out new looks and techniques

downforce (DOUN fors) – a downward aerodynamic pressure

grand prix (GRAHN PREE or GRAN PREE) – French words meaning "big prize"; the fastest racing series, like the modern Formula One

marque (MARK) – the logo for an automobile manufacturer or its models

monocoque (MAH no kok) – in vehicles, a body constructed with the frame as a single unit

production car (proh DUK shun KAR) – a car built for sale to the public

prototype (PROH tah tihp) – for carmakers, the first working model of a design

specifications (spe sih fih KAY shunz) – detailed design instructions or a list of these technical features

suspension (sah SPEN shun) – in a vehicle, the system of shock absorbers, springs, and other parts between the wheel and frame that smoothes the ride and increases control

torque (TORK) – a measure of mechanical strength or turning force

turbocharger (TUR boh char jur) – a special fan turned by the engine's exhaust gases that works to pump more air into the cylinders and boost power output

Further Reading

A&E Home Video. *Ultimate Autos – Bugatti* (History Channel), 2006.

Donovan, Sandra. *Sports Cars*. Lerner Publications, 2006.

Price, Barrie, and Jean-Louis Arbey. *Bugatti Type 44 & 49: The 8-Cylinder Touring Cars 1920-1934*. Veloce Publications, 2007.

Spurring, Quentin. *Grand Prix! Rare Images of the First 100 Years.* David Bull Publishing, 2006.

Zuehlke, Jeffrey. *Concept Cars*. Lerner Publications, 2007.

Websites

www.bugatti.com

www.bugattipage.com

www.bugatti-trust.co.uk

Index

About the Author

Tracy Nelson Maurer writes nonfiction and fiction books for children, including more than 60 titles for Rourke Publishing LLC. Tracy lives with her husband Mike and two children near Minneapolis, Minnesota.